TROLLEY BUSES

1913 THROUGH 2001
PHOTO ARCHIVE

William A. Luke

Iconografix
Photo Archive Series

Iconografix
PO Box 446
Hudson, Wisconsin 54016 USA

Library of Congress Card Number: 2001131938

ISBN 1-58388-057-7

01 02 03 04 05 06 07 5 4 3 2 1

Printed in the United States of America

Cover and book design by Shawn Glidden

COVER PHOTO: See page 110.

Book Proposals

Iconografix is a publishing company specializing in books for transportation enthusiasts. We publish in a number of different areas, including Automobiles, Auto Racing, Buses, Construction Equipment, Emergency Equipment, Farming Equipment, Railroads & Trucks. The Iconografix imprint is constantly growing and expanding into new subject areas.

Authors, editors, and knowledgeable enthusiasts in the field of transportation history are invited to contact the Editorial Department at Iconografix, Inc., PO Box 446, Hudson, WI 54016.

Table of Contents

ACKNOWLEDGMENTS

Photographs in this book are from the bus history library of the author, William A. Luke, unless noted as photo credits from other individuals and organizations.

The following persons and organizations were very helpful in providing information that has made this book possible.

Jim Boon, Vehicle Maintenance Manager, King County Department of Transportation, Seattle, Washington

Clarence Giuliani, Consultant, Dayton, Ohio

James Graebner, President, Lomarado Group, Denver, Colorado

Tom Jones, Librarian, Motor Bus Society, Clark, New Jersey

Steve Morgan, Trolley Bus Historian, Portland, Oregon

Peter Newgard, President, Canadian Transit Heritage Foundation, Gloucester, Ontario

Herb Pence, Consultant, Manchester, New Hampshire

Cliff Scholes, Trolley Bus Historian, Cincinnati, Ohio

Michael Voris, Supervisor, Transit Fleet Management Group, King County Department of Transportation, Seattle, Washington

Special mention should be made to the late Tom Van De Grift, who, for a number of years, presented many photographs (some of which are used in this book) to the library of William A. Luke and others.

In addition, the 1973 book *Transit's Stepchild, The Trolley Bus* by Mac Sebree and Paul Ward, was a valuable reference source, as well as a number of issues of the Motor Bus Society's *Motor Coach Age.* Information for several Boston, Massachusetts, pictures came from the 1970 book *Trackless Trolleys of Boston* by Bradley Clarke. The 2001 book *World Trolley Bus Encyclopaedia* by Alan Murray was a useful source of reference especially for the world trolley bus pages.

FOREWORD

by Clarence Giuliani

The history of the electric trolley bus (ETB) is more interesting to those who have had the pleasure to be a part of this mode of public transportation. Although most historians believe that any subject must have a substantial number of years of experience before it can be accurately observed, I will take the writer's prerogative to qualify for this authority, having been active in the operation and maintenance of trolley buses for more than 50 years—from 1948 to the present.

Probably the most significant change in the history of electrically driven mass-transit vehicles has been the disappearance of public transit systems owned by electric public utility companies. Most of the early trolley buses were modifications of internal-combustion-propelled, rubber-tired vehicles. Propulsion by direct current motors was the incorporation of a very practical and understandable power source for conversion, distribution, and ultimate controls by known and established technology in the form of direct current. The application of 600 or 750 Volts Direct Current (VDC) was shared by the use of this same power in many downtown office buildings and industrial facilities for elevators, cranes, and other electrical applications.

In recent years, the development of electronic control devices permitted the simplification of controls for acceleration, braking, and auxiliary devices. The elimination of mechanical contractors led to more efficient power systems that saved substantial amounts of empty-weight penalties. At the same time, however, the addition of the need for air conditioning systems, complex regulation of brake performance, the requirement for compliance with disability requirements, and other devices added more weight and complexity of design and maintenance.

One of the greatest impediments to the development of better ETB products has been the objection in local political circles to the aesthetic perception of the overhead-wire power-distribution systems. Requests for the retention and expansion of existing electric systems continued to decline over the period and caused the capital costs for the ETB systems in favor of using self-propelled vehicles, and in some cases, light-rail systems. This reduced, market-generated demand virtually destroyed the incentives for vehicle manufacturers to increase research and development to lighter-weight, more power-efficient vehicles. The advantages of ETB operations in the form of quiet performance, sufficient power for gradient (hilly) operations, and environmentally desirable characteristics have been far overwhelmed by the flexibility, capital and operating costs, and more familiar features of diesel and alternative-powered rubber-tired vehicles.

Despite the apparent lack of great public interest in ETB technology, the lingering nostalgia, and loyal support of trolley bus fans, there are still significant interests in such cities as San Francisco, Seattle, Dayton, Boston, and Philadelphia. Perhaps the impacts of energy conservation, environmental considerations, and support by city planners will continue to provide sufficient pressure to encourage and increase the use of electric trolley buses in future transportation plans.

Clarence I. Giuliani
Dayton, Ohio

INTRODUCTION

The electric trolley bus (ETB) is a passenger transportation vehicle very similar to a typical city bus. It has rubber tires, a front axle that steers, and a body like any other transit bus. But instead of an internal combustion engine, electricity from overhead wires powers the ETB. Two poles on top of the trolley bus collect the electricity from one of the overhead wires and return it to the grounded second wire.

The propulsion technology developed concurrently with the streetcar. Indeed, the earliest United States patent for a trolley bus was awarded in 1882, well before streetcars were a commercial success and, in fact, the trolley buses of the 1920s used street railway motors and controls. While the streetcar ran on its own rails and needed no steering capability, ETB technology did not become viable until paved highways and heavy highway vehicles became widespread. The fact that the trolley bus does not need a track gives it greater maneuverability, allowing it to pull into curb stops and then rejoin normal vehicle traveling lanes, or to pass double-parked vehicles.

There have been five eras for trolley bus systems in the United States and Canada. The first era lasted until the late 1920s and was marked by both technological experimentation and a search for the proper role for the ETB. Although a few early lines lasted for some years, only the Philadelphia installation has operated continuously since that time.

The second phase, which began with the Salt Lake City installation in 1928 and the Chicago commitment of 1930, featured wide adoption of the mode in the United States; mostly in small- and medium-size cities, and three early lines in Canada. This era was brought to a close by the onset of World War II.

The third era lasted for a decade after the end of the war. It was marked by strong growth in big city systems and a few new starts, mostly representing a substitution of ETBs for streetcars. However, several small systems converted their ETBs to buses during this time. Canadian properties reached their maximum number and size during this time.

By the mid-1950s, which marked the beginning of the fourth era, the seemingly irreversible decline in ridership, coupled with the need for a greatly expanded service area because of exploding sub-urbanization, caused most trolley bus systems to be converted to the ubiquitous diesel bus.

The modern era began in about 1990, and has been primarily in a holding pattern, with the few remaining established trolley bus systems replacing outdated vehicles and strengthening their operations. No new systems have been established in the United States or Canada in a half-century, and now, only Seattle, San Francisco, Dayton, Philadelphia, Boston, Edmonton, and Vancouver still operate trolley buses as part of their fleets.

The first trolley bus installations occurred in the early part of the twentieth century. The trolley bus that operated in the Laurel Canyon in the Los Angeles area in 1910 was the first revenue line in the United States. It lasted for only a few years. Merrill, Wisconsin, also had an early trolley bus service which ran from 1913 to 1915.

There were other more serious developments in the 1920s. Brill built some 21 Rail-less Cars for lines in Philadelphia, Baltimore, Petersburg (Virginia), and other cities. Other systems were built in Rochester, Staten Island and Cohoes, New York; Toronto and Windsor, Ontario; and Minneapolis, Minnesota. Except in Philadelphia, all were discontinued within 10 years. A number of short-lived demonstration lines were also tried during this time.

Salt Lake City's 1928 installation marked the beginning of trolley bus acceptance and expansion. It was widely heralded, and it played the same role for the trolley bus as Richmond, Virginia, had for the streetcar some 40 years before. The key breakthrough was the adaptation of the best of modern bus technology with the newest in electric motors and controls. Success spawned widespread imitation, and with the Chicago installation of 1930, the mode gained acceptance as a technological alternative to mainstream transit. The 1930s saw important growth for trolley bus services in some large cities, but mainly for small and medium urban areas. These were the Depression years, so the purchase of new streetcars to replace those from the turn of the century would have been very expensive. Also, extending streetcar lines within growing city and suburban areas would have meant expensive infrastructure costs. Automobiles were increasing in numbers. New roads were being built and existing streets were being improved. Power companies owned many of the transit systems. For these systems the trolley bus was a natural choice because ETBs made installation of tracks unnecessary and power companies could continue supplying electricity to run the vehicles. New trolley bus services were introduced in more than 40 U.S. cities and three cities in Canada prior to World War II.

In the 1930s, the two major builders of trolley buses in the United States were the J.G. Brill Company and the Pullman-Standard Company. These firms, along with St. Louis Car Company and Cincinnati Car Company, were established builders of rail cars. The growing market for trolley buses also attracted three experienced motor bus manufacturers: Twin Coach Company, Mack Trucks, and the Yellow Truck & Coach Manufacturing Company. Other firms such as Perley Thomas, ACF, MCI, and the British suppliers Leyland and AEC, produced small numbers of trolley buses for the United States and Canada.

After World War II there were a few new starts: Birmingham, Little Rock, Los Angeles, Dallas, and Johnstown. Some of the early systems, mostly single-route operations such as in Knoxville, Peoria, Fitchburg, and Rockford, converted their trolley bus lines to bus lines. The large fleet of All-Service Vehicles operated by Public Service of New Jersey was retired. Several large cities—Chicago, Atlanta, New York, Boston, San Francisco, Cleveland, Providence, and New Orleans to name a few—greatly expanded their trolley bus networks, and bought hundreds of new vehicles. In 1946, a new trolley bus manufacturer, Marmon-Herrington Company of Indianapolis, Indiana, began producing trolley buses in great numbers. Marmon-Herrington built 1,509 trolley buses for the United States in nine years between 1946 and 1955, making the firm the largest builder during the period. Pullman-Standard, Brill, St. Louis Car Company, and Twin Coach were also active in the market. However, Yellow Coach and Mack built no trolley buses after World War II. As was the case earlier, a few smaller builders produced single orders for trolley buses.

After World War II there were 12 new trolley bus systems started in Canada. A new manufacturer, Canadian Car & Foundry (CCF-Brill), located in Fort William (now Thunder Bay), Ontario, began building trolley buses in Canada. Between 1946 and 1954, CCF-Brill built 1,094 trolley buses in addition to its regular motor bus production.

As the 1950s progressed, transit ridership decreased. To make matters worse, transit companies had to expand their route networks into rapidly sprawling suburbs to keep their passenger base from dwindling further. Most companies, both public and private, decided to dispose of their electric transit operations. Motor buses were becoming the preferred vehicles for urban passenger service. Fuel was inexpensive, and buses also offered more flexibility at the time. By the end of 1975, there were only five U.S. cities and four Canadian properties operating trolley buses.

The last trolley buses of the postwar era for North American service were delivered by Canadian Car & Foundry in 1954 and Marmon-Herrington in 1955. The total number of trolley buses delivered in systems in the United States and Canada by the major manufacturers is as follows:

Manufacturer	Years Produced	Total Delivered
ACF-Brill *	1921-1952	2,129
Pullman-Standard *	1922-1952	1,877
Marmon-Herrington	1946-1955	1,509
St. Louis Car Company	1921-1951	1,119
CCF-Brill	1946-1954	1,094
Twin Coach Company	1928-1949	658
Yellow Truck & Coach **	1932-1938	456
Mack Trucks	1934-1943	291

*including subsidiaries
**including All-Service Vehicles

There was some activity in the trolley bus industry in the 1970s, mainly because trolley buses owned by the remaining systems required replacement. With all former domestic trolley bus manufacturers out of business there was concern about a source for new trolley buses. Flyer Industries of Winnipeg, Manitoba, Canada, indicated a willingness to produce new trolley buses. Toronto

Transit Commission was the first to acquire new Flyer trolley buses. Actually, only the bodies from Flyer were new—the motors were refurbished from previously owned trolley buses and installed in the new Flyer bodies. Hamilton Street Railway Company chose to do the same and worked out a plan similar to Toronto's, acquiring 40 bodies from Flyer Industries and using refurbished motors. Edmonton and Vancouver also bought new trolley buses from Flyer, but Edmonton's lasted only a few years before being replaced.

The remaining trolley bus systems in the United States also went to Flyer Industries, which had worked out an arrangement with the AM General Corporation to produce motor bus bodies. These bodies were also used for trolley buses. As a result, all five United States trolley bus systems added these new trolley buses and virtually all the older trolley buses were retired. Articulated trolley buses never became popular in the United States or Canada. But in 1987, Seattle Metro acquired 46 articulated trolley buses from MAN Truck and Bus Company in North Carolina. Flyer Industries later built 60 articulated trolley buses for San Francisco. In Canada, Edmonton Transit added 100 trolley buses from an electrical firm, Brown Boveri of Montreal. Bodies for these new trolley buses were built by the Diesel Division of General Motors in Canada.

Seattle had a strong commitment for trolley buses for some time. Because Seattle's downtown is geographically confined, a tunnel for trolley bus operation was completed in 1990. While many of Seattle's trolley buses were suitable for use within the tunnel, longer routes operating well beyond the tunnel would have required construction of new overhead wire. Instead, Seattle chose to acquire dual-mode trolley buses, which could operate as trolley buses in the tunnel and as diesel buses out of the tunnel. No domestic manufacturer was willing to build this type of trolley bus, so Seattle looked to overseas builders. Breda Construzioni Ferroviarie in Italy became the supplier of the new dual-mode trolley buses, with 236 units delivered in 1990.

In the late 1990s, Dayton chose to purchase 57 new trolley buses from ETI, a joint-venture partnership between the experienced Czech trolley bus manufacturer Skoda and the United States firm AAI. San Francisco has been updating its trolley bus fleet with 33 articulated and 240 standard trolley buses, also from the Skoda/AAI joint venture. Boston has ordered new Neoplan trolley buses for its Cambridge lines. Philadelphia will require a renewal of its trolley bus fleet soon, but no decision has been made.

Seattle's King County Metro has made an interesting trolley bus decision, reminiscent of that made by the Toronto Transportation Commission in 1969. King County Metro has ordered 100 bus bodies from the Gillig Corporation in Hayward, California. These bus bodies will be fitted with reconditioned motors from older trolley buses in the Seattle fleet. Seattle already has a large fleet of Gillig diesel buses.

Trolley bus operations in most of the world underwent declines and closures similar to North America. An exception to this has been Eastern Europe, where trolley bus operations are still abundant; in fact, more are planned. Russia has 89 cities with trolley bus systems; Ukraine has 48 and Belarus seven.

Western Europe, on the other hand, has seen trolley buses dwindle in number more like North America. Germany, once having 74 cities with trolley bus systems, now has only four. France had 34 systems at one time, but now has only six; Italy had 60 systems and now has 14. Great Britain had trolley bus systems in 49 cities and today there are none. Even Africa had 15 cities with trolley buses; now, none. Latin America had 36 trolley bus systems, and today is down to 13.

There has been new interest in some places for trolley buses. Quito, Ecuador, for example, launched a trolley bus system in 1995 with 54 articulated trolley buses that use an exclusive busway. Sao Paulo, Brazil, with 550 trolley buses, had an ambitious program for a guided trolley bus system with large-capacity bi-articulated vehicles.

In France, Irisbus and Matra Transport have begun producing a new vehicle based on the Civis system. It involves trolley bus-type vehicles on guided roadways. Also, Bombardier Transportation in France has a new trolley bus vehicle type that can operate on a guided or unguided roadway. The vehicles have rubber tires and overhead power, but auxiliary diesel engines allow them to operate off the overhead system.

Another trolley bus type of operation is planned for Trieste, Italy. It involves a system developed by Ansaldo Breda in Italy. Vehicles for the system are being supplied by Neoplan of Germany. The system does not require overhead wires, but electrical power is received from a trough in the roadway.

Trolley buses seem to be staging a revival, and with new developments and new vehicles those systems now in operation have a better opportunity to survive and may even spur new systems.

Merrill, Wisconsin, was one of the first cities in the United States to have a commercially operated trolley bus line. Merrill Railway & Lighting Company was the company that began the line in 1913 with one vehicle built by the Field Electric Bus Company. The trolley bus lasted in Merrill until 1919 when it was sold to an individual in Massachusetts. This pioneer trolley bus led the way to more trolley bus experiences in the 1920s. *Wisconsin Public Service Corporation*

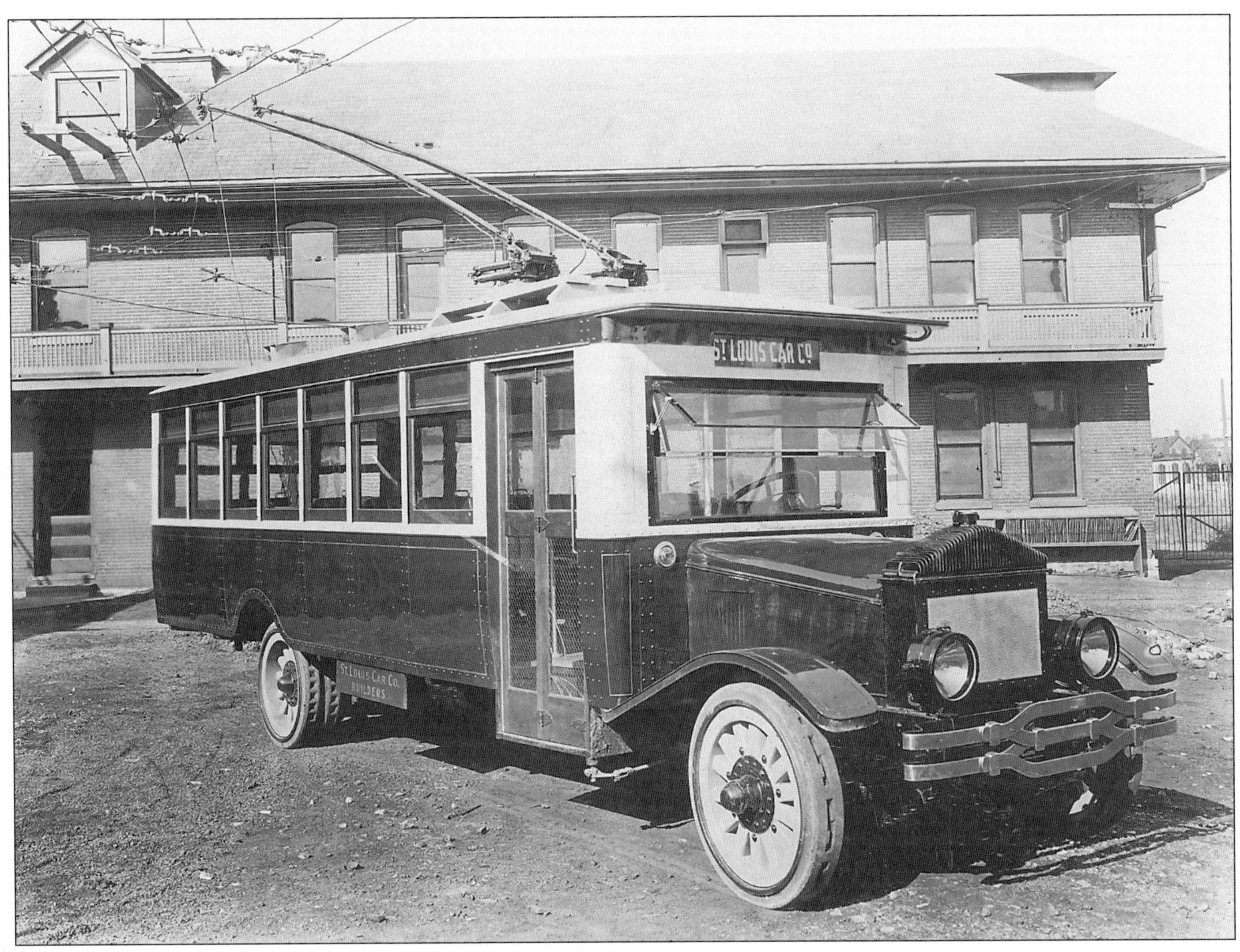

St. Louis Car Company was one of the earliest builders of trolley buses. Founded in 1887, it was an experienced builder of streetcars and other transportation vehicles. In 1921 the company produced its first trolley bus, called a Trackless-Trollicar. Four of them operated in Windsor, Ontario, and one of these even operated briefly in Detroit. Shown here is one of the demonstrators of 1921. It wasn't until 1930 that more modern trolley bus production began at the St. Louis Car Company. The company produced 1,119 units in its 30 years of trolley bus building.

This Atlas Trollibus was one of eight operated on New York's Staten Island for six years, beginning in 1921.

Twin City Rapid Transit Company of Minneapolis-St. Paul, Minnesota, built this one-of-a-kind trolley bus that operated in Minneapolis for one year, 1922-1923. A Brill Rail-less car was also used.

The first trolley buses to operate in Philadelphia were eight J. G. Brill Company Rail-less Cars like the one pictured here. Two other trolley buses were in the original fleet.

The Brockway Corporation built 16 trolley buses, five with Kuhlman bodies which operated in Rochester, New York, between 1923 and 1932 by the Rochester Railway Coordinated Bus Service. Rochester also converted seven Brockway motor buses to trolley buses in 1924-1925.

Capital District Transportation Company of Albany, New York, ran four trolley buses on a route in suburban Cohoes. Four of these Brockway trolley buses with Watson bodies ran from 1924 to 1933.

The ACF Company of Philadelphia tried to enter the trolley bus business in 1929, and built four units. This one ran in New Orleans for several years. After merging with Brill to become ACF-Brill, trolley bus production went to Brill plants, and ACF concentrated on motor buses.

The Utah Light & Traction Company of Salt Lake City launched one of the early trolley bus systems in the United States in 1928. The first 12 trolley buses were six-wheel vehicles built by the Versare Car Company of Albany, New York. In 1929, Utah Light & Traction Company added seven similar two-axle trolley buses, one of which is pictured here. These seven were built by Cincinnati Car Company, which had absorbed the Versare Car Company in 1928. The first Twin Coach 40TT trolley buses were also added in 1929, bringing the fleet total to 26 vehicles. The Salt Lake City trolley bus system closed in 1946.

The Tennessee Public Service Company began operating a small trolley bus service in Knoxville in 1930. Four Cincinnati Car Company trolley buses (one pictured here) entered Knoxville service at that time. When the system was fully depreciated, it was replaced with motor buses. The Cincinnati Car Company, which bought the Versare Car Company in 1928, only built 28 trolley buses of this type before closing down in 1931.

Soon after the inauguration of trolley bus service by the Chicago Surface Lines in 1930, six Brill 40-passenger vehicles from Brill's American Car Company in St. Louis entered service. They had two General Electric 298 motors, type PCM control, and CP-25 straight air-brake equipment. American was purchased by Brill in 1902 and became Brill of Missouri just before the Depression forced its closure in 1931. The plant turned out 31 additional trolley buses for Chicago, plus one demonstrator and four trolley buses for Rockford, Illinois.

A decision was made in October 1931 in Duluth, Minnesota, to replace some streetcars with trolley buses. Two Model T-40 trolley buses from Brill's Kuhlman plant in Cleveland, Ohio, were the first to go into service. In May 1934, just prior to the end of all Duluth streetcar service, the Duluth-Superior Transit Company added 16 more trolley buses; seven Brills and nine Twin Coaches. Duluth's trolley bus service ended in 1957.

A small trolley bus system, initially consisting of five 1931 Brill vehicles (one pictured here), was inaugurated by the Illinois Power and Light Company in Peoria, in 1931. Two St. Louis Car Company trolley buses were added in 1938. Only one transit line, Monroe Street in Peoria, was operated with trolley buses. In October 1946, 70 streetcars (which had remained in service) and the seven trolley buses, were replaced by a fleet of new General Motors diesel buses. The trolley buses were sold to the city of Des Moines, Iowa. *Motor Bus Society*

There have been two trolley bus operations in Massachusetts: a large one in Boston still in operation, and a smaller one in Fitchburg. Operated between 1932 and 1946 by the Fitchburg and Leominster Street Railway Company, the system had only seven T-40 Brill trolley buses. The first one, No. 101 (pictured here), served until the system shut down. *E. V. Warren Collection*

After World War II, Des Moines (Iowa) Railway converted its last streetcar line and increased its trolley bus fleet to 159. To replace the streetcars, 58 new ACF-Brill T-44 trolley buses were purchased between 1945 and 1948. In 1949, 27 ACF-Brill T-46 trolley buses were added. In addition, some used trolley buses from Peoria, Illinois, and Fitchburg, Massachusetts, were acquired. Pictured here is one of the seven 1932 Fitchburg Brill trolley buses, which was used only for trippers. All seven were built at Brill's Kuhlman plant. In Des Moines trolley buses were referred to as Curbliners.

Shreveport (Louisiana) Railways began a trolley bus system in 1931. Eventually, all transit routes in Shreveport were operated with trolley buses except one, which operated buses. The first five Shreveport trolley buses were T-30 Brills built at Brill's Kuhlman plant in Cleveland, Ohio. By 1936 there were 20 T-30 Brills in service, like the one shown here. Brill, of Philadelphia, Pennsylvania, built a total of 93 small 30-passenger trolley buses until 1937. Shreveport trolley bus service ended in 1965.

The St. Joseph (Missouri) Railway, Light, Heat and Power Company decided to replace streetcars with buses and trolley buses in 1931 after performance tests in revenue service of a streetcar, a gasoline bus, and a trolley bus on one route. A year later, five 29-passenger Brills, the first trolley buses for St. Joseph, except for a demonstrator that was retained, were delivered. The service expanded and in 1937, eight 40-passenger Model SM Brills (one pictured here) with General Electric motors, were acquired. The St. Joseph trolley bus system operated until 1966.

In 1937, Shreveport (Louisiana) Railways continued to replace streetcars by expanding trolley bus operations. This T-40 Brill trolley bus and six others were added in late 1936. In late 1937-early 1938, 17 more were purchased, and 11 T-40 SMT Brills entered Shreveport service in 1939. The final three Brills were purchased in 1940. A fleet of 58 trolley buses was in service in 1940. Shreveport trolley bus service ended in 1965. This photograph was taken in 1964.

One of the first trolley buses to enter service for the Des Moines (Iowa) Railway was this Model T-40S Brill. A fleet of 28 trolley buses was used in this initial Des Moines trolley bus service in 1938. In the next two years, three more T-40 Brills, 25 44SMT Brills, and four second-hand 30-passenger Brills from Topeka were added. Then in March 1942 the company placed an order with Brill, but World War II intervened, and not until 1945 did Des Moines get the first seven Brill postwar trolley buses built. Later, 78 more new Brills, plus second-hand trolley buses from Peoria, Illinois, and Fitchburg, Massachusetts, produced a peak system total of 159 trolley buses by 1950. Des Moines trolley bus service ended in 1964.

This Brill T-408 trolley bus, pictured on Huffman Avenue, was originally in the Peoples Railway Company fleet of Dayton, Ohio. It was acquired in 1939 when Peoples, originally a streetcar company, began converting to trolley buses. In 1945 the company was sold to Dayton's City Railway Company, later to be named City Transit. When this picture was taken in 1960, this 1939 Brill was in the City Transit colors and fleet. It was taken out of service in the mid-1960s. *Cliff Scholes*

In June 1940, trolley buses began replacing streetcars in Denver, Colorado. Initially, four Denver Tramways lines were converted to trolley bus routes with 45 Brill 44SMT trolley buses that were acquired that year. Pictured are two of the Brills at the end of Route 11. Just before World War II, 17 Brills were delivered. A further 80 Brills and 56 Marmon-Herrington trolley buses were added between 1948 and 1950. This brought the fleet of trolley buses to 208. Denver was a growing city with increased traffic in the 1950s. New one-way streets and other traffic changes, as well as higher electricity costs, brought an end to Denver trolley bus service in 1955. *Motor Bus Society*

During World War II, Honolulu (Hawaii) Rapid Transit Company had record ridership. Many of the passengers traveled on the system's 90 Brill trolley buses like the one pictured here. The Waikiki-Liliha line began in 1938 with the first 30 Brills. In 1941, Honolulu's last streetcars ran and 60 Brill T-44s were added. In 1944 these trolley buses ran 4 1/4 million miles and carried 44.5 million riders. After World War II, 25 more Brill trolley buses were acquired. Honolulu trolley bus service ended in 1957.

Trolley bus service was introduced in late 1941 in Akron, Ohio, by the Akron Transportation Company with 12 Brill Model 40 SMT vehicles, one of which is pictured here. The following year, 20 Twin Coach Model 44 GTT trolley buses entered service. After World War II, Akron ordered ACF-Brill trolley buses: 18 in 1945, 10 in 1947, and 10 more in 1948. This gave Akron a total of 70 trolley buses. This was one of the few trolley bus systems to use only Westinghouse motors for its vehicles. Akron's trolley bus service ended in 1959. *Motor Bus Society*

Indiana Service Corporation of Fort Wayne, Indiana, began trolley bus service in 1940 with 28 Brill 40 SMT vehicles. Forty others were added to the fleet in 1942, including the one pictured here at Calhoun and Washington Street five years later. The system added 10 ACF-Brills in 1946, but due to ridership declines, they were sold to Indianapolis in 1953 and resold to Dayton in 1956. Fort Wayne did not add any more trolley buses and continued to operate the 68 until the system closed in 1960. *G. Dengler, Cliff Scholes Collection*

Portland (Oregon) Traction Company decided to convert to trolley buses in 1935 and introduced a downtown demonstration loop. A Mack from Toledo, Ohio, and a St. Louis Car Company car from Columbus, Ohio, were the trolley buses tried out during this demonstration. As a result of the demonstration, trolley buses replaced several streetcar routes in Portland. The initial order for 120 trolley buses went to Mack. Twenty more Macks arrived in 1937 and one in 1940. One of the 141 Mack CR 38 trolley buses of 1938 is pictured here. Portland had the largest fleet of Mack trolley buses. The city's trolley bus operation ended in 1958.

From 1922 to 1931, United Railways & Electric Company in Baltimore, Maryland, ran a short trolley bus line as a suburban feeder using three Brill Rail-less vehicles. On March 6, 1938, the company reintroduced trolley buses on heavier trunk lines. The initial fleet consisted of 10 Brill T-40s and 11 Mack CR trolley buses, one of which is shown here. Baltimore Transit operated a maximum of 190 trolley buses during the 1948-1952 period. The system added 106 Pullman-Standards and 63 postwar Brills, but diesel buses replaced trolley buses in June 1959.

The Delaware Electric Company operated city transit in the Wilmington, Delaware, area from 1927 until 1941. That company began operating trolley buses in 1939 with 52 Brill 40-passenger Model 40 SMT trolley buses initially replacing most of the streetcar system. Three Macks (one pictured here) also entered service that year. Seventeen more Brill Model 40 SMTs were added in 1940, 1941 and 1942. The 72-trolley bus fleet lasted until February 1958.

The second acquisition of trolley buses by the Cincinnati, Newport & Covington Railway Company (CN&C) of Covington, Kentucky, was for 10 Mack CR3S trolley buses. They were the only Macks built for the company and were delivered in 1939 for use on the Ludlow Highway Line bus service. CN&C had started its trolley bus service in 1937 and eventually operated a total of 42 trolley buses. The trolley bus service ended in 1958.

Winnipeg (Manitoba) Electric Company began operating trolley buses in 1938. The first trolley buses were 11 Mack CR3S 30-passenger vehicles. Five more Macks assembled by Mack of Canada were added in 1940 and the five Macks pictured here were delivered in February 1943. Winnipeg Electric also had eight Pullman-Standards and a single Motor Coach Industries trolley bus by 1948. After that 104 CCF-Brills were purchased over several years. Winnipeg had a large trolley bus operation including 18 second-hand Pullman-Standard trolley buses from Providence and 10 ACF-Brills from Flint added in 1956. Trolley bus service in Winnipeg ended in 1970.

Southern Public Utilities, a large power company in the Carolinas that later became known as Duke Power Company, operated transit systems in seven cities. One of those cities was Greensboro, North Carolina, which began a 9.5-mile route with 12 trolley buses. Five were 1934 Pullman-Standard 34 C-96 29CX units, one of which is pictured here. These, and three others for one of the company's other trolley bus systems in Greenville, South Carolina, were the only 29-passenger trolley buses built by Pullman-Standard. Trolley bus service ended in both cities in 1956.

Trolley bus service was launched in Boston, Massachusetts, by the Boston Elevated Railway in April 1936 with six Pullman-Standard trolley buses. One of these trolley buses is shown here at the Bennett Street Carhouse. It operated the Harvard-Lechmere route. This trolley bus was scrapped in 1952.

One of the five Dayton, Ohio, trolley bus operators in the 1930s and 1940s was Oakwood Street Railway Company. The street railway was converted to trolley buses in January 1936. The 15 initial Oakwood trolley buses were 1935 Pullman-Standards (one pictured here) and were retired in 1959. They operated until the final consolidation of all Dayton trolley bus companies into City Transit in 1956. Oakwood was the last of the companies to be merged. *Cliff Scholes*

Dayton, Ohio, had five different companies operating trolley buses. In 1940, one of the companies operating trolley buses, Dayton Xenia Railway, purchased 12 40-passenger Pullman-Standard trolley buses, which were the company's first. One is shown here on Wyoming Street in 1955, the year the Dayton companies merged to become City Transit Company. Trolley bus service continues to operate in Dayton today. *Cliff Scholes*

In 1943, the Boston Elevated Railway took delivery of 30 Pullman-Standard 44-passenger trolley buses, one of which is pictured here at the Clarendon Hill Carhouse. With completion of this order there were 157 Pullman-Standard trolley buses and five Twin Coach trolley buses in the Boston fleet. Trolley buses in Boston were referred to as "trackless trolleys." This General Electric-equipped unit served until 1961.

By the outbreak of World War II, the Duluth, Minnesota, streetcar system had been converted to either bus or trolley bus operation. A fleet of 29 Brill and Twin Coach trolley buses—all General Electric equipped—was in service. The war brought dramatic ridership increases and the company was able to obtain authorization from the Office of Defense Transportation to order three trolley buses in 1943. Since only Pullman-Standard was permitted to build trolley buses at the time, and only in limited numbers, Duluth was fortunate to obtain three of the 25 trolley buses built for five properties. The Duluth Pullman-Standards (one pictured here) arrived in April 1944 and continued in operation until May 1957 when trolley bus service ended in Duluth.

The Seattle (Washington) Transit System received 15 Pullman-Standard 41-passenger trolley buses in 1943. The following year 15 more were delivered. These latter Pullman-Standards were originally ordered for the Columbus and Southern Ohio Electric Company by the Office of Defense Transportation. This brought the Seattle trolley bus fleet to a total of 307, the largest in North America at the time.

Edmonton, Alberta, began its trolley bus service in 1939. The first six trolley buses ordered by Edmonton Radial Railways were three-axle Leylands from England. In 1942, three British AEC, and in 1943, three Mack trolley buses, were added. Two wartime orders were placed with Pullman-Standard, each for eight trolley buses. One delivered in the first group is pictured here traveling downhill to the Low Level Bridge over the North Saskatchewan River. All Pullman-Standards were retired in 1966, but this unit—renumbered No. 113—has been preserved. Trolley bus service continues in Edmonton today.

Chicago Surface Lines operated many makes of trolley buses. Included were six St. Louis Car Company units, one of which is pictured here after delivery in 1930. They were the first trolley buses built by St. Louis except for four that went into service for one year, in 1921, in Detroit, Michigan, and in Windsor, Ontario. In 1931, Chicago Surface Lines was the largest trolley bus operation in the United States with 114 vehicles, and by 1937 had grown to 152 trolley buses. Eventually, the fleet expanded to 679 trolley buses at the end of 1952, the largest in North America. Chicago bought a total of 719 trolley buses over the years.

This St. Louis Car Company trolley bus—No. 22, delivered in 1932—was the last in a fleet of 22 trolley buses that operated the entire transit system of the Wisconsin Gas and Electric Company in Kenosha, Wisconsin. These St. Louis Car Company trolley buses had only one door, an unusual feature for trolley buses. Kenosha Motor Coach Company had taken over the city transit service in 1947, three years before this photo was taken. Non-electric buses replaced all of Kenosha's trolley buses in 1952.

This Twin Coach Model 40TT was one of two vehicles to inaugurate trolley bus service in Brooklyn, New York, by the Brooklyn & Queens Transit Corporation (B&QT) in July 1930. The other trolley bus was an ACF. Six new Pullman-Standard trolley buses brought the B&QT fleet total to eight trolley buses. B&QT had this small trolleybus operation until 1948, when it gave the St. Louis Car Company an order for 200 trolley buses. The system continued until 1960.

Of the 90 Model 40TT trolley buses built by the Twin Coach Company prior to World War II, 58 went to the Chicago Surface Lines in 1930 and 1931. The last of five orders was a group of 10, which had 40 seats and two Westinghouse 1426 motors. Pictured here is one of these trolley buses, almost new, in service on the Belmont-Pacific line. At the end of 1931, the Chicago system was the largest in the country, with a 114-vehicle fleet consisting of 58 Twins, 37 Brills, 11 St. Louis Car Company cars, six Cincinnati-Versares and two ACFs. *George Krambles Archives*

The Youngstown (Ohio) Municipal Railway Company began trolley bus service December 8, 1936, with 25 Model 44RTT Twin Coach trolley buses. More Twin Coach trolley buses were acquired for Youngstown in each succeeding year until 1942, for a total of 54 vehicles. One of the first 1936 Twin Coaches is pictured here. Eight new Brills were acquired in 1945, and 10 Marmon-Herringtons were later added. Retirement of the trolley bus fleet began in 1956, with the last day of service being June 10, 1959. *Motor Bus Society*

Seattle (Washington) Transit System began trolley bus service in August 1940 when streetcar replacement began. The last cable car operation had just ended, and remaining streetcar service ended in 1941. An order placed by Seattle Transit at that time for 135 Twin Coach Model 41 GWFT trolley buses was the largest pre-World War II trolley bus acquisition by any property. One of the 1940 Twin Coaches is pictured here. At the beginning of World War II, Seattle had a fleet of 307 trolley buses. This trolley bus fleet remained intact until 1962. A few Twins continued to run until 1971.

Trolley bus service in Kansas City, Missouri, was started in 1938 by the Kansas City Public Service Company with 34 Mack trolley buses. Eight more Macks were added in 1941 replacing streetcars on two lines. In 1940, a fleet of Twin Coach Model 44 GWFT trolley buses had entered service allowing further conversions. A number of these Twin Coaches are pictured here at the Kansas City Municipal Stadium awaiting the end of the ball game. For a brief time, from July 1948 until January 1954, Kansas City Public Service operated interstate trolley bus service between Missouri and Kansas. The trolley bus service in Kansas City ended in 1959.

Twin Coach Company was one of the most innovative manufacturers of buses and trolley buses during the 1920s and 1930s. Among these innovations were four articulated vehicles, one of which, a trolley bus built in 1940, is pictured here. The articulation was only in the vertical direction but the rear axle was steerable. Cleveland (Ohio) Railway Company operated this "Super Twin" in demonstration service in 1941 and then purchased it for $17,500 in early 1942. It ran in Cleveland until 1954. Interestingly, the back part of this bus was reserved for smokers. *Motor Bus Society*

Yellow Truck and Coach Manufacturing Company, a division of General Motors Corporation, entered the trolley bus building business in 1932. The first customer was the Wisconsin Gas and Electric Company of Kenosha, Wisconsin. The order was for 12 Model 701 MT-A trolley buses. At the time Kenosha had 19 streetcars and 11 buses. The Yellow Coach trolley buses, along with 10 from St. Louis Car Company, operated all the transit service in Kenosha—the only U.S. city to have only trolley buses operating its urban transit.

Public Service of New Jersey operated a large network of transit lines throughout New Jersey. In the 1920s, a large fleet of buses was acquired, many of them gas-electrics. In 1934, an experimental bus known as an All-Service Vehicle (ASV) was developed, capable of operating electrically under wire but also having a 450-cubic-inch gasoline engine to allow it to run off wire. After successful testing, Public Service ordered 61 Model 729 ASVs from Yellow Truck and Coach Division and a single Mack in 1935. In 1936, 296 more Model 729 Yellow Coach ASVs with gasoline auxiliary engines were acquired by Public Service, followed by one diesel version in late 1935. Public Service also converted 226 Yellow Coach gas-electric buses of 1936 and 1938 vintage to ASVs. The entire ASV fleet was gone by 1948.

In 1937, streetcars in Flint, Michigan, were replaced with 46 Yellow Coach Model 737 trolley buses, the prototype shown here. These vehicles were unusual because they were 104-inches wide and had dual General Electric traction motors mounted behind the rear axle. Flint Trolley Bus Company was the largest purchaser of Yellow Coach trolley buses, with the exception of ASVs for Public Service of New Jersey. After World War II, five Brills were added in 1946, 15 in 1948, and 15 more in 1951. Ten Brills were sold to Winnipeg in 1956. These were later resold to Mexico City, making them the only trolley buses to operate in the United States, Canada, and Mexico. All of the Yellow Coach trolley buses were withdrawn in 1956 in favor of diesel buses.

The only Yellow Coach trolley bus in the Baltimore (Maryland) fleet was No. 2501, built as an ASV. It was delivered in 1938 when Baltimore decided to reinstate trolley buses, and was the only Yellow Coach Model 729 in the initial purchase of 22 trolley buses. Yellow Coach built 356 ASVs for Public Service of New Jersey; the Baltimore ASV was the only other one. It was made a straight trolley bus in 1944 and was retired in 1953.

Other than the 356 Model 729 ASVs, Yellow Coach trolley buses were only operated by five properties—The Milwaukee (Wisconsin) Electric Railway and Transport Company was one. In November 1938, 40 of the Yellow Coach Model 1208s (one pictured here) went into service. The first 20, including this one, had a single General Electric motor while the last 20 had Westinghouse motors—the only Westinghouse-equipped trolley buses built by Yellow Coach. These trolley buses were designed by TMER&T engineers in conjunction with Yellow Coach. Trolley bus service began in Milwaukee in 1936 and ended in 1965, with the largest fleet size being 400 vehicles from 1948 through 1955.

In 1937, Montreal Tramways Company was the first Canadian company to introduce trolley bus service except for the short-lived system in Windsor, Ontario, from 1922 to 1926, and a brief experience with trolley buses in Toronto from 1922 to 1925. Seven three-axle trolley buses, including one (pictured here) from the Associated Equipment Company (AEC) in Southall, England, began the Montreal service on the Beaubien line in 1937. The AEC vehicles had British Metro-Cammell-Weymann bodies and English Electric motors, and were retired between 1949 and 1951. Trolley bus service in Montreal expanded in 1947 but ended in 1966.

After an exhaustive study of transit-vehicle options in the late 1930s, Seattle decided to modernize its transit system by replacing its worn-out streetcar system with buses and trolley buses. Two large orders were placed for trolley buses in November 1939. Pacific Car & Foundry Company received one of the orders for 100 trolley buses. PC&F negotiated a license from Brill and one complete trolley bus was delivered from the Philadelphia plant. The other 99 buses, which were Model 40 SMTs, were built by PC&F. The Brill was the very last of that model built in the company's Philadelphia plant. All the Brills had General Electric motors. The other order was for 135 Twin Coaches which were delivered at the same time but with Westinghouse motors. One of the PC&F-Brills is pictured here. These trolley buses had a long life, with the last one being retired in 1964.

This one-of-a-kind trolley bus, Model TRY with Westinghouse equipment, was built by Motor Coach Industries in Winnipeg, Manitoba, in 1942. It went into service for the Winnipeg Electric Company and operated until 1960. Motor Coach Industries, primarily a builder of inter-city coaches, built only one unit because of a scarcity of materials and high import duties on traction motors. Trolley bus service in Winnipeg began in 1938 with an initial fleet of eight Mack trolley buses, which quickly grew to 16. All trolley bus service in Winnipeg ended in 1970.

In 1959, in order to keep trolley bus service operating, St. Joseph (Missouri) Light and Power Company decided to purchase some used trolley buses. These would replace three-fourths of its trolley bus fleet, which was predominantly pre-World War II vintage. After evaluating available units the company bought 15 ACF-Brill trolley buses with General Electric equipment from Wilkes-Barre which had just ceased its trolley bus operation. These refurbished trolley buses ran until 1966, when all trolley bus service ended after 34 years. Trolley bus No. 278, ex-Wilkes-Barre No. 841 of 1946, is pictured on St. Joseph's South Park line.

The longest continuously operating trolley bus operation in the United States is in Philadelphia, Pennsylvania. The first Philadelphia trolley buses purchased in 1923 were nine 28-passenger Rail-less Cars built by the J.G. Brill Company in Philadelphia. In 1924 an unusual four-motor ex-demonstrator built by the Trackless Trolley Corporation was added. Another Brill Rail-less Car arrived in 1930. These trolley buses operated for many years until being replaced in 1935 when Philadelphia Rapid Transit Company bought eight T-30 30-passenger trolley buses from the Brill Company. In 1941, 50 Brill 40SMT trolley buses were acquired and 10 more in 1942. In 1947, 65 ACF-Brill TC-44 trolley buses were purchased; the last in the group is pictured here.

The Cincinnati, Newport & Covington Railway Company of Covington, Kentucky—popularly known as the Green Line—started trolley bus service in 1937 with 21 Brill TC-40s following a disastrous flood that destroyed many streetcars. In 1952, six ACF-Brill units with single motors were purchased, one of which is pictured here. These were the last trolley buses built by Brill. Interestingly, the system was one of two interstate trolley bus operations, crossing the 1966 suspension bridge across the Ohio River between Kentucky and Cincinnati. Trolley buses did not operate on Cincinnati streets, but operated directly into the Dixie Terminal. Green Line trolley bus service ended in 1958.

Calgary, Alberta, began its trolley bus operations in 1947 when streetcar replacement began. At that time 30 T-44 CCF-Brill trolley buses, like the one pictured here, were purchased. In the following three years 51 more were added. CCF-Brill had the franchise to build ACF-Brill buses and trolley buses in Canada at a factory in Fort William (now part of Thunder Bay), Ontario. Another four trolley buses were purchased in 1953 and delivered in 1954, the year CCF-Brill ended trolley bus production. Interestingly, as Calgary grew rapidly in the mid-1950s, its trolley bus service had to be extended and increased. As a result, 20 ACF-Brill trolley buses were acquired from Baltimore (Maryland) Transit in 1957. Calgary's trolley bus service ended in 1975.

Transit service in Port Arthur, Ontario, (now known as Thunder Bay after amalgamation in 1970 with neighboring Fort William) was operated exclusively with streetcars until 1947. At that time a fleet of eight CCF-Brill trolley buses was ordered by Port Arthur Public Utilities, but the order was increased to 10 before the first line opened. Port Arthur also operated a joint service with Fort William Utilities. The trolley bus service ended in 1971, soon after the formation of Thunder Bay Transit. The Port Arthur trolley bus bodies were scrapped, and the motors and controls were salvaged and sold to Hamilton for use in their new Flyer trolley buses.

New Year's Day 1947 saw the inauguration of trolley bus service in Kitchener, Ontario. Ten CCF-Brill T-44 trolley buses (one pictured here) went into service on King Street. Other than a demonstrator later sold to Cornwall, these were the first production CCF-Brill trolley buses. Five more CCF-Brill trolley buses were added in the next few years. Kitchener Public Utilities Commission purchased five used trolley buses from Ottawa, Ontario, in 1959, increasing Kitchener's fleet to 21 vehicles. The City of Kitchener took over the system in 1973 and named it Kitchener Transit. Trolley bus service ceased soon afterward.

In 1949, the Cornwall (Ontario) Street Railway, Light, and Power Company purchased 15 CCF-Brill T-44 trolley buses to replace an obsolete fleet of streetcars. A similar CCF-Brill demonstrator was added in 1952. By 1970, only four Cornwall trolley buses were in operation, and later that year the trolley bus service was discontinued. Cornwall was the smallest North American city to have a non-experimental trolley bus system.

The Ottawa Transportation Commission (OTC) was formed just prior to the purchase of 10 CCF-Brill TC48A trolley buses in 1949 to replace streetcars that dated from 1916. The streetcars had been built by the Ottawa Car Company, a sister company to the OTC. The new trolley buses cost slightly more than $25,000 each. In 1959, the OTC abandoned its electric operations and replaced the remaining streetcars and the 10 trolley buses by adding 107 General Motors diesel buses to its existing fleet. Ottawa's trolley bus system lasted less than eight years, the shortest life of any North American trolley bus system after World War II. *City of Ottawa Archives, CA-1687*

Trolley bus service by the Regina (Saskatchewan) Municipal Railway had an interesting beginning. A decision was made in 1947 to begin replacement of an aging streetcar fleet. Twenty CCF-Brill trolley buses were acquired by late 1948. On January 23, 1949, a bitterly cold day, a fire destroyed the car barn. The fire consumed 17 new trolley buses, nine of the 12 gasoline buses, and 14 streetcars. In order to restore full service as soon as possible, buses of various kinds were rented and a rush order for trolley buses was placed. Several Canadian cities deferred their orders so Regina Municipal Railway could receive its trolley buses within a few months. The trolley bus pictured here is from the rush order. Regina took delivery of eight more CCF-Brill trolley buses in 1950, when the last streetcars were retired. The trolley buses continued in service until 1966.

In March 1949 the Nova Scotia Light and Power Company (NSL&P) of Halifax began replacing streetcars with trolley buses. There were 65 CCF-Brill T-44 trolley buses which entered service in Halifax at that time. Six more were purchased in 1949. NSL&P added four more CCF-Brills in 1950, two in 1952, and four in 1954. The total fleet of CCF-Brills was 81. One of the CCF-Brills is pictured in 1964 on the new Angus L. MacDonald Suspension Bridge. Six used Pullman-Standard trolley buses purchased from Providence, Rhode Island, were added in 1955. Halifax had the distinction of having all its routes operated by trolley buses. The service ended in 1969.

Vancouver, British Columbia, began trolley bus service in 1948 with 82 CCF-Brill T-44 units. In 1949, 86 T-48SP CCF-Brills were delivered, one of which is pictured here when it was operated by BC Hydro, the operator of Vancouver city service at the time. In 1950, 88 more CCF-Brill T-48s went into service. The following year, 55 CCF-Brill T-48As were added, and in 1954 the last 16 CCF-Brill trolley buses built went to Vancouver. In all, Vancouver purchased 327 CCF-Brill trolley buses, almost one-third of all that were built. Trolley bus service continues in Vancouver, but all of the CCF-Brills have been retired.

Fort William, Ontario (now known as Thunder Bay after amalgamation in 1970 with neighboring Port Arthur) was the location of the first Canadian trolley bus manufacturing plant, the Canadian Car & Foundry Company (CCF-Brill) plant established in 1945. CCF-Brill buses and trolley buses were built under a franchise from the ACF-Brill Company in the United States. A total of 1,094 trolley buses were built between 1946 and 1964. Originally, Fort William Utilities bought eight in 1947 and two more (one pictured here) in 1951. The 10 Fort William trolley buses ceased service in 1971 when Thunder Bay Transit was formed.

Trolley bus service in Montreal, Quebec, began in 1937 with seven British AEC trolley buses. Montreal Tramways had a major expansion of trolley bus service in 1947 when 40 CCF-Brill T-44s were purchased. In 1950 another 40 CCF-Brill T-44s were added, followed in 1952 by the last order of 25 CCF-Brill T-44As, one of which is pictured here. Montreal ceased trolley bus operation in 1966, and all but three of the CCF-Brill trolley buses were sold to Mexico City.

In 1946, Marmon-Herrington began building trolley buses in this 100,000-square-foot plant in Indianapolis, Indiana. In 1955, the last Marmon-Herrington trolley bus was built for the United States. The company did build 110 more trolley buses, but they were exported to Brazil. There were 1,509 trolley buses—five different models— built for 18 U.S. cities in the nearly 10 years of domestic production. Many Marmon-Herringtons were resold, several times in some cases.

Indianapolis, Indiana, had trolley bus service for almost 25 years, from December 1932 to 1957. Indianapolis Railways bought 15 T-40 Brills with two motors and a rear-exit door to begin the service. In 1934, 80 more two-motor T-40 Brills with center exits were delivered. That was the largest single order for trolley buses, at that time, placed by any U.S. property. An additional 57 Brills entered service in 1937, 1941, and 1942, bringing the fleet total to 162. After World War II, Indianapolis Railways turned to Indianapolis-based Marmon-Herrington Company to modernize the trolley bus fleet. Indianapolis was one of the largest operators of trolley buses for many years. Through 1952, 75 Marmon-Herringtons were purchased, including the very first one, pictured here.

The Milwaukee (Wisconsin) Electric Railway and Transport Company (TMER&T) began trolley bus service in 1936. At the end of World War II, the fleet numbered 279 trolley buses supplied by Twin Coach, St. Louis Car Company, Pullman-Standard, and Yellow Truck & Coach Division. Trolley bus No. 328 (pictured here) was one of a second group of trolley buses built by Marmon-Herrington in 1946. The 26 trolley buses delivered were then joined by 74 Pullman-Standards and 26 more Marmon-Herringtons in 1948, making the system one of the largest in the country. Although Milwaukee bought only 52 new Marmon-Herrington trolley buses, 90 more were acquired from Indianapolis to replace older units. The Milwaukee trolley bus era ended in 1965.

74

Columbus was one of seven Ohio cities with trolley buses, the first going into service in December 1933 for the Columbus and Southern Ohio Electric Company. Pre-World War II trolley buses in Columbus were Brills, with the exception of 18 units built by St. Louis Car Company. In 1947, 83 44-passenger Marmon-Herrington trolley buses were purchased followed by 55 48-passenger Marmon-Herringtons in 1948. A 1947 Marmon-Herrington is seen on a downtown Columbus street in this photo. Streetcar service ended when these trolley buses entered service. Trolley buses, later operated by Columbus Transit, lasted until 1965.

Shreveport (Louisiana) Railways added to its fleet of 71 trolley buses in 1947 with the purchase of 18 Marmon-Herrington T-48 units, the fifth of which is shown here. The rest of Shreveport's fleet consisted mainly of various sizes of Brills, plus four Pullman-Standards. The Marmon-Herringtons and 12 ACF-Brills were the only new trolley buses acquired by the company after World War II. In 1952 and 1956, 18 Little Rock trolley buses were added to replace 1930-vintage units. Trolley bus service ended in 1965 when American Transit Corporation became the new operator of the Shreveport transit service.

San Francisco was one of the few cities in the United States to have more than one company operating trolley buses simultaneously. The Market Street Railway began a single line in 1935 and the San Francisco Municipal Railway followed in 1941. The companies merged in 1944. A 24-vehicle order in 1948 brought San Francisco its first Marmon-Herrington trolley buses. These trolley buses (one pictured here) were the only 40-passenger TC-40 trolley buses built by Marmon-Herrington. San Francisco Municipal Railway eventually operated 274 Marmon-Herrington trolley buses.

Formed in 1945, the Chicago Transit Authority (CTA) became an operating system when it acquired Chicago Surface Lines' streetcar, bus, and trolley bus routes, and later the Chicago Rapid Transit operation. When the trolley bus service came under the CTA, there was a fleet of 152 vehicles. Because of CTA's strong interest in trolley buses, a number of new routes were established. Older vehicles were being replaced and in 1950 CTA ordered 359 Marmon-Herrington T-48 trolley buses, one of which is pictured here. Delivery began in April 1951 and continued through May 1952. This order was the largest by any system in trolley bus history. Even with the retirement of some 1930-1931 trolley buses, Chicago had a fleet of 679 units by the end of 1952, the largest-ever trolley bus fleet in North America. Trolley bus service in Chicago ended in 1975.

Two 1951 Marmon-Herrington Model TC-49 trolley buses of Cleveland (Ohio) Transit System are shown at the Dupont Loop at 105th Street and Dupont Avenue in 1959. Trolley bus No. 1298, at the curb, is in Cleveland Transit's original paint scheme. Trolley bus No. 1305 is in the blue-and-white paint scheme being adopted at that time. Cleveland operated 124 Marmon-Herrington trolley buses, 50 of which were the last new trolley buses purchased. Cleveland also bought used trolley buses: 32 Brills from Louisville and 50 Pullman-Standards from Providence. Between 1945 and 1953 the Cleveland trolley coach system grew from 29 to 461 vehicles, but the service ended in 1963. *Ed O'Meara, Cliff Scholes Collection*

Dallas (Texas) Railway & Terminal Company began trolley bus service in November 1945 with 30 ACF-Brill TC-44 vehicles equipped with General Electric motors. Another order for 24 ACF-Brill TC-44 trolley buses was delivered in 1947. The last new trolley buses for Dallas were 16 Marmon-Herrington Model TC-48s arriving in November 1951. In 1958-1959 a boxy air conditioning unit was added to 50 of Dallas' 80 trolley buses. One of the 1951 Marmon-Herringtons with the new air conditioning unit is pictured here. In 1953, Dallas added 10 used Marmon-Herringtons from Cincinnati.

Trolley buses operated in Little Rock, Arkansas, for just under nine years. Capital Transportation Company, a subsidiary of the Arkansas Power and Light Company, began the trolley bus service in 1947. Capital Transit Company, a new company, became the operator of Little Rock's trolley bus system in 1952. Difficulties, including a strike in 1956, resulted in the company surrendering its franchise. The new company decided against operating trolley bus services. The last trolley bus ran in Little Rock in 1956. Little Rock's trolley bus fleet had 29 ACF-Brill T-44s, and six TC-48 Marmon-Herringtons (one pictured here) in 1954. Dayton purchased 11 of the ACF-Brills and the Marmon-Herringtons.

Philadelphia is the oldest continuously operating trolley bus system in North America, having started in 1923. With the exception of an ex-demonstrator built by Commercial Truck Company in 1923 and a group of six wartime Pullman-Standard trolley buses, the fleet was built entirely by the hometown firm Brill until 1949. In that year, and again in 1955, the city of Philadelphia purchased two groups of Marmon-Herrington trolley buses which were leased to the Philadelphia Transportation Company. Trolley bus No. 303, a TC-49, shown here in 1961 at the Frankfurt Avenue City Loop, was one of 43 from the 1955 order that was Marmon-Herrington's last domestic order for trolley buses. *Cliff Scholes Collection*

Georgia Power Company in Atlanta inaugurated trolley bus service in 1937 with 27 Twin Coach 40 RWFTT trolley buses. Although additional Twin Coach units were acquired in the following years, Pullman-Standard trolley buses became the primary choice. Georgia Power Company had the distinction of having the world's first air-conditioned trolley bus. It was No. 1234, the last of a group of six Pullman-Standards delivered in July 1945. The 100 Pullmans ordered in August of that year were intended to be equipped with air conditioning but the technology for such units was not reliable, as No. 1234 soon demonstrated.

Trolley bus service in Birmingham, Alabama, didn't begin until 1947, and the system lasted only 11 years. Birmingham Electric Company's fleet consisted of 148 Pullman-Standard trolley buses and was the only all-Pullman-Standard fleet in the country. The first order for 40 was delivered in 1946 and 1947, and the second group of 45 followed six months later. A third order for 69 vehicles was placed in 1946, but owing to financial constraints, deliveries did not occur until later; 49 arrived in 1951 and 14 in 1952. Slight differences between Pullman-Standards can be seen here by comparing No. 107 from the first order with No. 222 from the last order. Most of the fleet was sold when service ended in 1958, with 24 going to Vancouver and 58 to Mexico City.

This Pullman-Standard trolley bus was the last of a fleet of 45 acquired by City Transit in Dayton, Ohio, in 1947. These were the last new Pullman-Standards to be acquired by City Transit, which was the surviving identity of transit in Dayton after the five trolley bus companies were consolidated. City Transit also bought 30 new Marmon-Herrington trolley buses—10 T-44s in 1947 and 20 T-48s. In addition, the system acquired used Marmon-Herringtons from Oakwood, Little Rock, Kansas City, Cincinnati, and Columbus. By 1956, City Transit had absorbed the other trolley bus systems operating in Dayton. *Cliff Scholes Collection*

In 1945, Georgia Power Company of Atlanta operated 113 trolley buses, of which 48 were Twin Coach, 31 St. Louis Car Company, and 34 Pullman-Standard. An order for 100 more Pullman-Standard trolley buses was placed in 1945, but wartime shortages stretched out the delivery into 1947. The trolley bus pictured here was one of the last 40 delivered. They were Westinghouse equipped. Sixty more Pullman-Standard, 40 ACF-Brill, and 140 more St. Louis Car Company trolley buses followed for a total fleet of 453, making the Atlanta system one of the largest in the country. Atlanta's trolley bus service ended in 1963.

By 1949, the United Electric Railway of Providence, Rhode Island, was operating a fleet of 310 trolley buses, several of which are shown here at Exchange Place. Almost all of Providence's trolley buses were Pullman-Standards built at the Osgood Bradley plant in nearby Worcester, Massachusetts. Trolley bus service in the area began in 1931 in Pawtucket with four Brills followed by 15 more Brills. The first Pullman-Standard, an ex-demonstrator, arrived in 1934. With the exception of one final order for 13 Brills in 1935, all trolley buses from then on were Pullman-Standards. Trolley buses in Providence were referred to as "trackless trolleys." A change in management in the early 1950s led to the end of the trackless transit system in 1955. Seventy of the Pullman-Standards were converted to gasoline or diesel buses.

This Pullman-Standard trolley bus was the first of 90 delivered in 1951 to the Metropolitan Transit Authority formed in 1947 to serve the Boston area. The picture was taken at the Arborway Carhouse. There was a door on the left side of these trolley buses so they could be used for unloading transfer passengers at the Harvard Square Station. Boston continued to acquire Pullman-Standard trolley buses after World War II, and added 243 of them between 1947 and 1951. Those delivered in 1951 were the last domestic orders for Pullman-Standard trolley buses.

New Orleans (Louisiana) Public Service Company had one of the early trolley bus services in the United States, beginning in December 1929. A Twin Coach 40TT trolley bus was the first one in service along with an ACF. Prior to World War II there were only nine trolley buses in New Orleans. In the postwar years, 154 St. Louis Car Company trolley buses went into service, including this 1948 unit shown on Canal Street. New Orleans also had 49 Marmon-Herrington trolley buses. The fleet peaked at 212 trolley buses from 1952 to 1955. Service ended in 1967.

Cincinnati (Ohio) Transit acquired this St. Louis Car Company 44-passenger trolley bus (pictured on Linn Street) in a 30-vehicle order in 1948. These were added to a previous order for 30 trolley buses from St. Louis Car Company delivered in 1947. Trolley bus service in Cincinnati was launched in 1936 by the Cincinnati Street Railway Company with seven Mack CR 40-passenger trolley buses and 10 Twin Coach 41 RWFT trolley buses. Although there was a variety of trolley buses operating in Cincinnati, the majority of the buses (214 units) were Marmon-Herringtons. Trolley bus service ended in 1965. *Cliff Scholes Collection*

The last trolley buses delivered to Atlanta's Georgia Power Company in 1948 and 1949 were 140 St. Louis Car Company units. These trolley buses had new styling with slanted sides above the belt line, large windows with sliding sashes, a wide fluted aluminum belt, and other features. These trolley buses were the only ones of this type built. This addition to the Atlanta fleet brought the total number of trolley buses to 453, the largest trolley bus fleet in the United States at that time. Trolley bus service in Atlanta ended in 1963.

The Detroit (Michigan) Street Railway Company conducted two trolley bus demonstrations during the 1920s and operated a single route with six Twin Coach trolley buses from 1930 until 1937. The next Detroit trolley bus experiences came in 1949 and 1951, when two heavy streetcar lines were converted to trolley bus service. Sixty Twin Coaches were purchased in 1949, the last trolley buses built by Twin Coach. Then, in 1951, 80 St. Louis Car Company STL-48 trolley buses were delivered, one of which is pictured here. The fleet continued in service until November 1962.

The last new-start trolley bus system in the United States was by the Johnstown (Pennsylvania) Traction Company in November 1951. Six St. Louis Car Company 48-passenger trolley buses, one of which is pictured here, went into service. Johnstown later added Marmon-Herrington and ACF-Brill trolley buses from Wilmington, Delaware, and the Cincinnati, Covington and Newport Street Railway, both of which had abandoned trolley bus service. At its peak Johnstown had 27 trolley buses, but its trolley bus service ended in 1967.

Kenworth Motor Truck Corp. of Seattle, Washington, built buses as early as the late 1920s and for a short time after World War II. In 1948, Portland (Oregon) Traction Company ordered 50 of these 45-passenger Kenworth trolley buses, the only ones of any size built by the company. When Portland's trolley bus service ended in 1958, only 31 of the Kenworths remained.

Twin Coach Company delivered 90 post-World War II trolley buses (one pictured here) to the San Francisco (California) Municipal Railway in 1949. It was the largest postwar order for trolley buses received by Twin Coach. These trolley buses, which ran until the mid-1970s, seated 44 passengers and had a Westinghouse 1442 motor. The San Francisco trolley buses, and the 60 that went to Detroit in 1949, were the last to be built by Twin Coach.

In 1967, the Toronto (Ontario) Transit Commission had 153 trolley buses, which were showing their age. Two trolley buses went out for remanufacture, one to Western Flyer Coach, Ltd. (Flyer Industries, Ltd.) and the other to Robin-Nodwell, an English firm. Satisfied with the Flyer product, Toronto contracted for 151 new bodies, installing electrical gear from its own CCF-Brill trolley buses plus salvaged electrical equipment from CCF-Brill trolley buses purchased from Ottawa, Halifax, and Cornwall. These vehicles, including the one pictured, were completed in 1971 and were the first new trolley buses in North America since 1955. Toronto's first trolley bus line was a short feeder opened in 1922 using four vehicles, but ended in 1925. In 1947, Toronto again began trolley bus service, which continued until 1993. *Toronto Transit Commission*

The Hamilton (Ontario) Street Railway Company began trolley bus service December 10, 1950, with 18 CCF-Brill units, followed by 30 more a year later. In 1972, after a demonstration of Toronto's first Flyer trolley bus, Hamilton ordered 40 similar vehicles at a cost of $1,750,000. Motors and controls for these trolley buses were salvaged from Hamilton's retired CCF-Brill units and from a group of similar vehicles purchased from Thunder Bay when that system shut down in 1972. The Flyer trolley bus pictured here was the first of the 1972 delivery. Hamilton's trolley bus service ended in 1992.

Over the years, five separate companies operated trolley buses in Dayton, Ohio. All were eventually merged into City Transit, which in turn became publicly owned in 1972. In 1971, City Transit had purchased a new Flyer trolley bus in an effort to show that a modern trolley bus was a practical alternative for Dayton. After considerable debate, Miami Valley Regional Transit Authority, the new public operator of transit in Dayton, awarded a contract to Flyer for 64 new E800 trolley buses in January 1975. The new trolley buses were delivered, but debate on the future role of the trolley bus continued. The smallest city in the country to have trolley buses continues to operate them.

In 1976, the Massachusetts Bay Transportation Authority (MBTA) in Boston bought 50 Flyer Industries, General Electric trolley buses to replace older vehicles. This Flyer, No. 4034, is shown at the Auburn Street entrance to the Harvard Station Busway in Cambridge, in January 2000. The Flyer trolley buses are due to be replaced with new Neoplan trolley buses.

From a peak fleet of 202 trolley buses in 1955, which included every Philadelphia trolley bus built after 1940, the Philadelphia Transportation Company began retiring trolley buses in 1959. By 1978, the remaining fleet was between 23 and 30 years old. A new fleet of 110 AM General trolley buses was ordered a year later. Shown here is AM General trolley bus No. 850 at the Bensalem end of Route 66. The Southeastern Pennsylvania Transportation Authority now operates five trolley bus routes, with about half of the AM General fleet still in active service.

Vancouver, British Columbia's, Metro Transit Operating Company purchased 246 Model E902 trolley buses from Flyer Industries in 1982. These trolley buses, like the one shown here, replaced older vehicles and are still in operation. Vancouver began its trolley bus system in 1947 and is the largest trolley bus system in Canada. *Bill MacDonald*

This articulated trolley bus is a French Renault PER 180 dual-mode. It went into experimental service for Seattle METRO in 1983, and was returned to the builder in 1984. Its traction motor was built by TCO, and had a Renault 6-cylinder 245-horsepower auxiliary diesel engine. Because Mack Trucks in the United States is 20 percent owned by Renault, this trolley bus was being demonstrated by Mack.

The German firm Maschnenfabrik Augsburg-Nuernberg AG (MAN) entered the United States transit bus market in 1976. A joint venture with the AM General Corporation was formed, which began building articulated buses. MAN later formed the MAN Truck and Bus Corp. and began building buses and trolley buses in a new factory in Cleveland, North Carolina. The company built 46 articulated trolley buses for Seattle (Washington) Metro in 1987. The 64-seat trolley buses (pictured here) have Siemens motors and controls.

Trolley bus service in Edmonton, Alberta, had started in 1939. In 1981 and 1982, Edmonton Transit took delivery of 100 new trolley buses. The new trolley buses were a product of Montreal-based Brown Boveri of Canada, which furnished the electrical and operating equipment. The bodies were built by Diesel Division of General Motors Corporation in Canada. These bodies were almost identical to the popular General Motors New Look diesel buses. In addition to promised energy savings from the new trolley buses, the bodies had parts that were interchangeable with Edmonton's diesel buses. In the years since the arrival of these trolley buses in Edmonton, there have been many changes. While 62 are still operating, 38 are for sale.

A transit tunnel under downtown Seattle was opened in 1990. Because of Seattle's geography the downtown has a very narrow width. Congestion was relieved by operating transit vehicles through the tunnel with several downtown stations. It was designed for trolley buses. New trolley buses, 236 units like the one pictured, were acquired from Breda Construzioni Ferroviarie in Italy, the only company to submit an acceptable bid. These Breda articulated trolley buses have AEG Westinghouse motors and a Detroit Diesel 6V-92 diesel engine. The buses operate as trolley buses in the tunnel and as diesel buses on the surface. Shown here is a Breda trolley bus just entering the tunnel, and one inside the tunnel (inset).

In 1993, San Francisco (California) Municipal Railway bought 60 New Flyer Model E-60 articulated trolley buses, the first articulated trolley buses built in Canada by New Flyer Industries. San Francisco Municipal Railway used these new trolley buses to replace older vehicles in the fleet. Trolley bus service continues in San Francisco today. *Bill MacDonald*

Dayton, Ohio's, Miami Valley Regional Transit Authority began taking delivery of 57 new trolley buses in 1998. The trolley buses are a product of Skoda, a large trolley bus manufacturer in the Czech Republic, and AAI, a subsidiary of United Industrial Corp. The joint venture of the two firms is named Electric Transit Inc. (ETI). Pictured here on Dayton's Main Street in September 1999 is one of the new trolley buses soon after delivery.

With its mid-1970s Flyer trolley buses wearing out, San Francisco Municipal Railway (Muni) asked for bids in 1996 for 220 two-axle and 30 articulated trolley buses. After a lengthy process, a contract was awarded to the firm ETI that is currently working with Skoda in the Czech Republic for the new trolley buses. Following an extensive prototype-testing program, production began, and the order was increased to 240 two-axle models. Shown here is the prototype ETI/ Skoda trolley bus in the Muni livery. *James Graebner*

The San Francisco Municipal Railway (Muni) originally ordered 30 articulated trolley buses from the ETI/Skoda joint venture. The order has been increased to 33 articulated units. Pictured here is the prototype ETI/Skoda articulated trolley bus. Both the standard models and the articulated models will come with most of the new gadgetry that is becoming more common in transit fleets. Global Positioning Satellite tracking, video cameras, and auxiliary power for off-wire travel are being installed on the new trolley buses. *Bill MacDonald*

Seattle, Washington's King County Department of Transportation implemented a unique solution when it determined 100 of its AM General trolley buses of 1979 needed replacement. Rather than buying completely new trolley buses, the decision was made to refurbish the motors of the old trolley buses and install them in new bodies. Gillig Corporation of Hayward, California, is building 100 bodies for the new trolley buses. The motors are being refurbished by the Alstrom Transportation Company. The first Gillig/Alstrom trolley bus is shown here in June 2001.

110

Drammen, Norway, began operating trolley bus service in 1909, which continued until the late 1960s. A 1910 Schiemann trolley bus refitted with pneumatic tires is pictured.

Stockholm, Sweden, began trolley bus service in 1941. In 1947 through 1951, these Scania Vabis trolley buses with Hagglund bodies are seen operating on Stockholm routes. Trolley bus service in Stockholm ended in 1964.

111

The Railways Economiques de Liege Seraing et Extensions S.A. in Belgium took delivery of four unusual three-axle, double-end Brossel trolley buses in 1936.

In Liege, Belgium, the Liege Seraing operation began trolley bus service in 1930. Two small, unique double-end Brossel trolley buses entered service in 1938.

This 1938 Tatra T-86 trolley bus operated in Prague, Czech Republic. Prague had trolley bus service from 1936 to 1972, and is considering reinstating trolley buses in the future.

One of the oldest continuously operating large trolley bus systems in Europe is in Milano, Italy. It began in 1933, and in 2001, 136 were in the fleet. Pictured here is one of 25 Fiat trolley buses acquired by the Milano company in 1951-1952.

In 1932 Lausanne, Switzerland, began what has become a large trolley bus system. Pictured here is one of the 32 FBW, Eggli-bodied trolley buses, acquired in 1937. Lausanne has a fleet of 113 trolley buses as of 2001. The Lausanne system is the oldest continuously operated trolley bus system in Europe.

Leoben, Austria, had trolley bus service from 1949 to 1973. Pictured here is a Graf & Stift trolley bus that was added to the small fleet in 1955.

London Transport had one of the world's largest trolley bus fleets with a peak of 1,811 vehicles. It was in operation between 1931 and 1962. Pictured here are two Leyland double-deck trolley buses in 1955.

This trolley bus operated in Adelaide, Australia, in the 1950s. It had a J. A. Lawton & Sons body with a British Sunbeam chassis. Trolley bus service in Adelaide began in 1937 and ended in 1963.

In 1951, the transit operator, AMDET, in Montevideo, Uruguay, purchased 18 of these British Park Royal-bodied trolley buses. At one time 358 trolley buses operated in Montevideo. The trolley buses were discontinued in 1992.

Johannesburg, South Africa, had trolley buses in service between 1936 and 1984. These 86-passssenger double-deck British BUT trolley buses were added to the Johannesburg fleet in 1957-1958.

In the year 2000, 18 Berkhof low-floor articulated trolley buses were delivered to the trolley bus system in Arnhem, Netherlands. The Arnhem system is operated by the contractor, Connexion, but the traditional Arnhem blue livery has been retained.

In 1987, Ghent, Belgium, ordered 20 Van Hool AG 280T articulated trolley buses for a new trolley bus service in that city which began in 1989.

New low-floor Graf & Stift trolley buses were delivered in 1995 to the system that operates transit service in Eberswalde, Germany.

Esslingen, Germany, acquired Mercedes-Benz duo-mode trolley buses in 1995. These vehicles operate as trolley buses within the city area, but are powered by diesel engines when they are in outlying areas.

Pictured is one of the 10 Russian-built ZIU-9 trolley buses operating in Debrecen, Hungary. The system opened in 1985 and these trolley buses went into service two years later.

Murmansk, Russia, on the Barents Sea, has had a trolley bus system since 1962. These ZIU Russian-built trolley buses have been a part of the 118 trolley bus fleet. *Ole Iskov*

It is interesting to note that trolley bus service was inaugurated in Gdynia, Poland, in 1943, during World War II. In 1995-1996 new Jelcz trolley buses were acquired for Gdynia services.

The trolley bus service in Chomutov, Czech Republic, is quite new, starting in 1995. At that time 25 Skoda 15 Tr articulated trolley buses were in service.

Limoges, France, began operating trolley buses in 1943. In 1983, 15 Renault Model ER 100 H trolley buses, like the one pictured, were acquired.

Trolley buses have been operating in Valparaiso, Chile, since 1952. At that time, six Pullman-Standard trolley buses were the last built by this company in the United States. These trolley buses, one pictured here, continue in service in 2001 after almost 50 years.

Zurich, Switzerland, began a trolley bus service in 1939. In 1988-1989, 35 of these Mercedes-Benz trolley buses were added to the fleet.

Naples, Italy, has two trolley bus operators, and one, Azienda Napoletana Mobilita, began taking delivery of 87 AnsaldoBreda low-floor trolley buses in the year 2000. One is pictured here.

The Societe Electrique Vevey-Montreux (VMCV) operates what could be called an interurban trolley bus line. VMCV serves a number of cities along Switzerland's Lake Geneva. Trolley buses were introduced in 1957, and in 1995 18 Van Hool articulated low-floor trolley buses were acquired, replacing all of the previously operated trolley buses.

Bombardier Transportation French Division has developed a new vehicle which could be classified as a trolley bus but it is also referred to as a "tram on tires." Shown here is one of the bi-articulated units operating test service on Paris' Trans Val de Marne line. It is dual mode with electrical power from an overhead wire and road track and two diesel engines.

A Marcopolo trolley bus, commemorating 50 years of trolley bus service in the city, is pictured in downtown Sao Paulo, Brazil. It is one of 500 trolley buses that serve the metropolis.

Sao Paulo, Brazil, is building a guided bus way called the Fura Fila for the operation of bi-articulated Marcopolo/Volvo trolley buses. The prototype trolley bus pictured is on display at the 1998 Expo Bus Exhibition in Sao Paulo.

The Municipality of Quito (Ecuador) built an exclusive bus way for trolley buses in 1995-1996. A fleet of Mercedes-Benz articulated trolley buses with Spanish Hispano Carrocera bodies were delivered in 1995-1996 to operate the service. Pictured here is one of the first 54 units. *Steve Morgan*

Trieste, Italy, is constructing a new trolley bus system which receives electrical power, not from overhead wires, but from a trough in the roadway. Neoplan low-floor articulated dual-model trolley buses similar to the one shown here would be used. AnsaldoBreda has developed the system.

A Word from the Author

Left to right: Michael Voris, Supervisor, Transit Fleet Contract Management Group; William A. Luke, book author; Jim Boon, Manager, Vehicle Maintenance and Terry Williams, Chief of Electronics. Voris, Boon and Williams are from the King County Department of Transportation in Seattle, Washington.

I developed a keen interest in bus transportation when I was quite young. I collected timetables, maps, publications, books, and what ever I could find about bus transportation. I also visited many bus operations and rode buses often.

As time progressed, I became employed in the bus industry. Later, I founded the bus *industry* trade journal, *Bus Ride.* After the publishing company was sold, I have continued writing articles and books about bus transportation, and I have also traveled frequently.

There have never been a great number of trolley buses in this country or elsewhere. Motor buses have always been found everywhere in great numbers. Because of the uniqueness of trolley buses and their presence in only a few cities, I took a special interest in them.

One of the smaller cities operating trolley buses was Duluth, Minnesota. I lived near Duluth and I would go there several times a year. Riding trolley buses that were operated there was always a pleasant experience.

After I spent a few years in the army during World War II, I began traveling quite often. Some of the cities where I observed and rode trolley buses in the late 1940s and 1950s were San Francisco, Denver, Milwaukee, Chicago, Kenosha, and Winnipeg. At the time, I took pictures of trolley buses whenever I could, and some pictures I took more than 50 years ago are pictured in this book.

In 1947, I also had the opportunity to see trolley buses in production; it was when I was in Fort William, Ontario, and visited the CCF-Brill factory. Fort William and neighboring Port Arthur had new trolley bus systems about the same time, and I pictured and rode their trolley buses.

In the late 1950s and 1960s, it was evident that trolley buses were losing their favor in many cities in the United States and Canada. So that I could get pictures and ride trolley buses before they disappeared, I visited a number of trolley bus cities. As a result, I made trips to St. Joseph and Kansas City, Missouri; New Orleans and Shreveport, Louisiana; Little Rock, Arkansas; Memphis, Tennessee; Birmingham, Alabama and Atlanta, Georgia. I also visited most Canadian trolley bus cities.

In more recent years, I traveled to many foreign countries and stopped to see trolley bus operations in a number of cities. The systems in Switzerland, Austria, Italy, and the Czech Republic have been especially interesting. I also observed trolley bus systems in Istanbul; Cairo; Wellington and Dunedin, New Zealand; the Baltic countries; Greece, Hungry, and Poland, as well as several places in South America.

New trolley bus developments have been of great interest. I had the opportunity to see the new rubber-tired tram (also classified as a trolley bus) being tested on the Val d' Marne line in suburban Paris. In Sao Paulo, Brazil, I have seen the four-axle, prototype Marcopolo/Volvo trolley bus, its test track, and the actual guided route under construction for a large new trolley bus system. The new Trieste, Italy, "Stream" system by AndalsoBreda has also been observed. In addition, I am interested in the new Quito, Ecuador, trolley bus system operating on an exclusive roadway, but I haven't seen it as yet.

I am pleased that I have been able, with the assistance of many friends, to author this Trolley Bus Photo Archive Book. By having this book published I am able to share many interesting pictures of trolley buses together with interesting stories about them and their systems written in the captions.

I have also authored or co-authored four other Photo Archive Books about buses. In addition, the book *Bus Industry Chronicle,* which I wrote, has an in-depth history of the bus industry in the United States and Canada, including trolley buses. There are many pictures. Hopefully more books about bus industry subjects will be forthcoming.

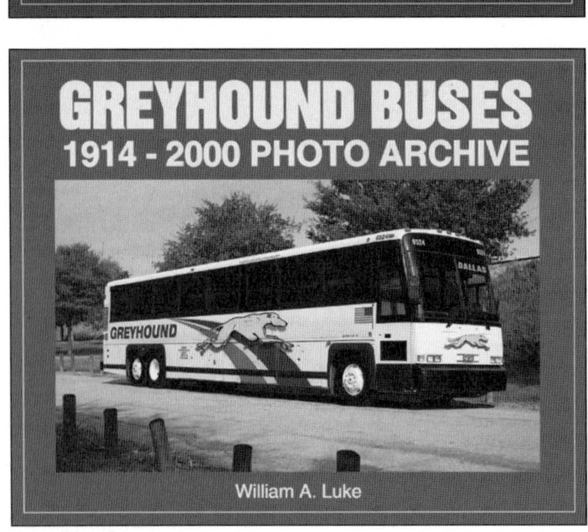

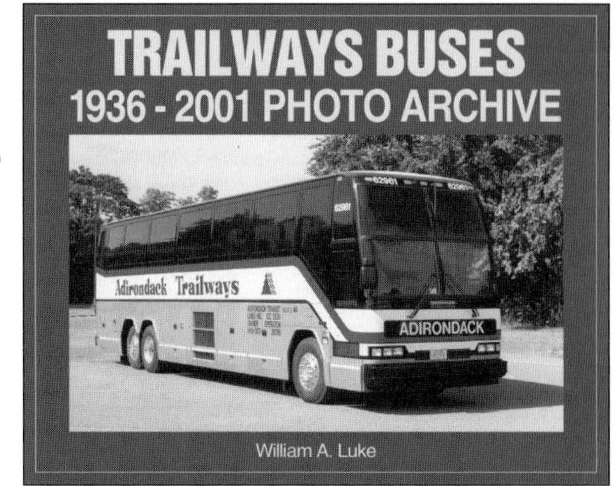

MORE GREAT BOOKS FROM ICONOGRAFIX

THE GENERAL MOTORS NEW LOOK BUS PHOTO ARCHIVE   ISBN 1-58388-007-0

TRAILWAYS BUSES 1936-2001 PHOTO ARCHIVE   ISBN 1-58388-029-1

MACK® BUSES 1900-1960 PHOTO ARCHIVE*   ISBN 1-58388-020-8

BUSES OF MOTOR COACH INDUSTRIES 1932-2000 PHOTO ARCHIVE   ISBN 1-58388-039-9

GREYHOUND BUSES 1914-2000 PHOTO ARCHIVE   ISBN 1-58388-027-5

FLXIBLE TRANSIT BUSES 1953-1995 PHOTO ARCHIVE   ISBN 1-58388-053-4

YELLOW COACH BUSES 1923-1943 PHOTO ARCHIVE   ISBN 1-58388-054-2

*This product is sold under license from Mack Trucks, Inc. Mack is a registered Trademark of Mack Trucks, Inc. All rights reserved.

ICONOGRAFIX, INC.
P.O. BOX 446, DEPT BK,
HUDSON, WI 54016
FOR A FREE CATALOG CALL:
1-800-289-3504

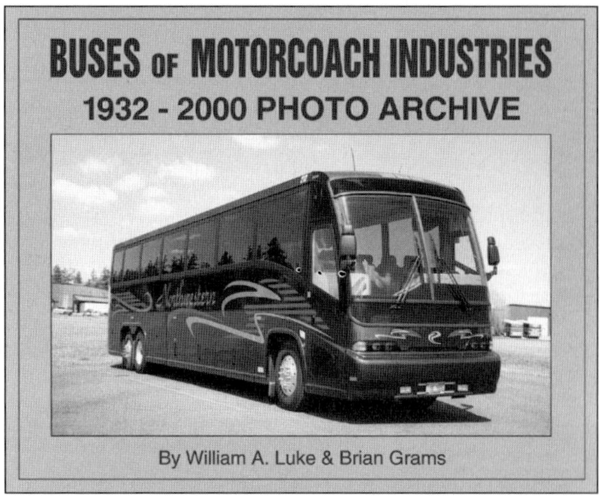

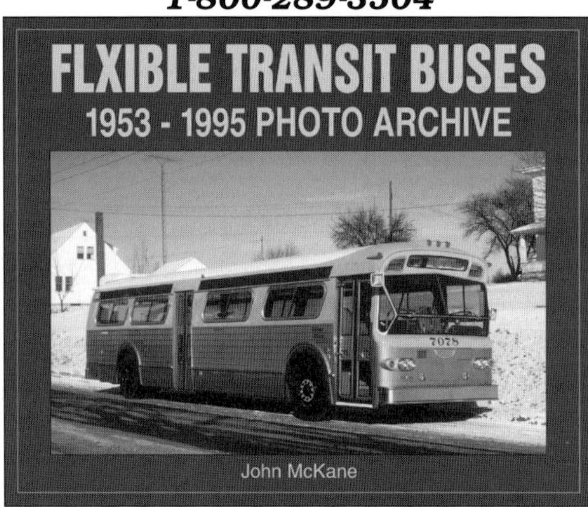

MACK® BUSES
1900 - 1960 PHOTO ARCHIVE
Edited by Harvey Eckart

GREYHOUND BUSES
1914 - 2000 PHOTO ARCHIVE
GREYHOUND
William A. Luke